The Ant and the Grasshopper:
A Response from the Left

Merrill Ring

Political Works:

Edited: ***Pithy Progressive Polemics***

Edited*: **Leftward Ho! (Corrected Edition)***

Philosophy Books:

Beginning With the Pre-Socratics

Philosophy Papers:

See: www. independent.academia.edu/MerrillRing

The Ant and the Grasshopper:

A Response from the Left

Merrill Ring

ISBN-13: 978-1544701028
ISBN-10: 1544701020

First edition 2017

Preface

There is an economic and sociological imagination at home in the writings of the political left. Those writings typically feature statistics both in criticism of opponents and in the development of positive views.

I have absolutely no objection to that mode of argument. But it is not the only way to go about expressing one's views and offering criticism of competing positions. For what it omits is the fact that *outlooks*, *perspectives*, *ideologies*, are not grounded in statistics. Having numbers thrown at you does not therefore make you change your mind on such basic matters, though they might make the exponent of an outlook uncomfortable. Numbers do not touch the outlook, the world view and its elements.

So frequently a different mode of argument is employed: personal narratives by people affected by policies. We are urged by politicians and political organizations to submit our stories of how such and such has affected or would affect us personally.

I seem to be much less moved by that technique than others. I keep asking myself 'But that is about me, that is only my story not that of others who are in similar boats.

Still, it is not necessary to be driven back to statistics by that shortcoming in the personal narrative mode of criticism. For there is something else that can be done.

That other manner of proceeding is to look with a critical eye at the world view itself – to notice the assumptions built into it, to discover the conflicts that it contains, to see how it fails to respond to quite ordinary but relevant facts.

It is that manner of criticism that I shall be indulging in here. I shall take Aesop's well-known fable of *The Ant and The Grasshopper* as a text that expresses a conservative world view and subject it to examination. I am not interested in numbers or in personal stories. I am interested in what that particular expression of a certain outlook amounts to and criticizing it from a quite different perspective.

The fable has been around a long time – and others, more closely related to my own persuasion, have in a wide variety of ways rejected its point of view. (To get a grasp of how the fable has been treated both by supporters and by critics down the centuries, the substantial Wikipedia article 'The Ant and The Grasshopper' is an excellent piece.)

But so far as I know, no one has gone about criticizing the fable in the same manner as I do here. I have found no literature in which the fable is taken apart piece by piece and examined.

I could have conducted this analysis at greater length. But I think that a decent brevity will be welcomed by most readers.

Note: there is yet another way of criticizing the *The Ant and the Grasshopper*: that is by telling an alternative story. For those who might want to pursue that line, I recommend Somerset Maugham's short story 'The Ant and the Grasshopper', John Updike's short story 'Brother Grasshopper' and John Ciardi's poem 'John J. Plenty and Fiddler Dan'.

An earlier version of this essay was originally published in the online journal Progressive Democracy (www.taipd.org).

The Ant and the Grasshopper:

A Response from the Left

If Aesop the slave did write the fable of *The Ant and The Grasshopper*, he would today be rightly labeled a conservative, a darling of the right-wing. For there is no doubt that the tale favors the ant, who labors hard all summer, laying in food for the winter, while the grasshopper enjoys himself; but come the winter the grasshopper needs the good will of the ant - who refuses to give it.

For centuries now, the fable has been used by conservatives (by whatever name they called themselves) to justify their ways and attitudes.

There is an up-to-date version of the fable (2008) made familiar in right-wing circles by one of their favorite pundits, Michelle Malkin. So the importance of the fable is not old history – it still speaks to the conservative mind.

My aim in this essay is to subject the entire fable to criticism from the left. The object is to negate Ant worship, though of course it is unlikely to be successful in accomplishing that. The outlook and attitudes expressed in the fable are too deeply entrenched in conservative thought to be eradicated easily.

The fable creates a world in which there are only two beings: an ant and a grasshopper. It opens: *"Once there lived an ant and a grasshopper in a grassy meadow."*

We progressives (or social democrats or modern liberals (not the neo-liberal variety)) must criticize those very opening words of the fable. For its aim is precisely to eliminate the social background of human life and to make its moral point as if ants and grasshoppers, and so too human beings, are fully formed atoms without regard to their fellow creatures and their institutions.

The ant in the fable does not live in an anthill, as do all other ants, and so has no culture to form it and no fellows to support it. It is a self-made ant. And equally the grasshopper is to be taken to be cultureless, to be free of any influences on its way of life not deriving from its own natural being.

That is, whatever good or bad accrues to them will be solely and totally a matter of their own doing. Ant is that paragon of the right, the self-made man who owes nothing to anybody else or to the social world (and even the natural world) into which it is born and develops. The Self-made Ant/Human Being is a product solely of his own self and especially his own effort. Grasshopper, on the other hand, is a lazy lay-about, who could have been providing for his own well-being but instead prefers to do nothing but enjoy himself: no one else is around to share his responsibility for his life and his problems. For the conservative, he is a self-made failure.

One of the basic tenets of modern liberalism or social democracy (or whatever the outlook is called) is that that picture of human atoms whose characteristics are not at all shaped by others or by the social world in which they find themselves is totally false. It is disagreement about that picture that creates a fundamental division between conservatives and social democrats.

It is tempting to turn to the important topic of just why modern liberals reject the individualistic assumptions of conservative social theory, to remind ourselves of why it is important to see people as social beings. (The topic today goes under the heading of *the social conditions for freedom* in the political philosophy, political theory, literature.) But that will have to wait for later. Ants and grasshoppers are the topic here.

In any grassy meadow, except the one in the fable, there is not a solitary ant and a solitary grasshopper. In fact, since ants are highly social and cooperative creatures, even more organized than we liberals can accept as a model for human life, Aesop's fable must be restructured from the start. Something like: 'In a grassy meadow was an ant colony. In the morning, the scouts went out to determine where the ants should spend the day. A straw boss assigned crews to various parts of the meadow and each unit went off to perform its day's work, bringing food back to the communal larder in the colony.' Now *that* would be a promising start to the fable.

In Aesop's version of the fable, however, Ant is alone in the grassy meadow (ignoring for now the grasshopper), having no friends or family, no fellows, no institutional framework, no history. What kind of life does she (or he) have? Work.

All day long the ant would work hard, collecting grains of wheat from the farmer's field far away. She would hurry to the field every morning, as soon as it was light enough to see by, and toil back with a heavy grain of wheat balanced on her head. She would put the grain of wheat carefully away in her larder, and then hurry back to the field for another one. All day long she would work, without stop or rest, scurrying back and forth from the field, collecting the grains of wheat and storing them carefully in her larder.

It is impossible to understand the conservative hatred (yes hatred) for welfare, for transfer payments to the unemployed, especially to those with long-term unemployment but even to those who have a shorter spell out of work, without understanding the conservative attitude toward work. And that attitude is best expressed in the tale of the ant. So do not take the above passage, which is the picture of Ant's life and labors, lightly.

The conservative's aim in the fable is to express first that the ant is virtuous without blemish and in that excellence owes nothing to anyone else (except perhaps implicitly to the farmer, who is not a conservative on this matter since he does not insist that every grain of wheat is rightfully his because he has produced it). Moreover, the ant is to be taken as the model of the good human life. What does the ant do? Work. Work in this picture is what it is to be human.

Further there is a conception of *what work is* that is embodied in the ant's story, especially in the paragraph above, a conception that is pure conservative doctrine. Work, what life is all about on this view, is incessant, repetitive and uninteresting in itself: in a word, work is grim drudgery. And as work is the core of life, life is ....

The dwarves' song 'Just whistle while you work' is complete anathema to conservatives. It is impossible, they hold, to be cheerful in work and life – or if you are, as are the dwarves, that is false consciousness, an attempt to hide from oneself the reality of what it is like to live and work.

But is work really incessant, repetitive and uninteresting?

That is an accurate description of what it was like, and is like, to work on an orthodox assembly line, say in a Henry Ford factory. The autos being assembled come past you on the line and you have one and only one task: to see that nut N is put on bolt B as each auto moves on down the line as they do inexorably. And you have to rise early in the morn, at least six days a week, and put in a ten hour day doing nothing but putting nut A on bolt B, with no breaks except a brief lunch stop. That is how you spend your life for, say, 40 years.

There are three things that must be said in reply to the conservative story: much work is not like being on an old-fashioned line, is not like the ant's labors; secondly, that contrary to the conservative view, it is possible to make things better, to improve the nature of work and thus our lives, to make our labors unlike the ant's; third it is possible to diminish the extent of work in our lives so we do not live like the ant but can create a fuller and richer human life.

Let me point out one further thing about the fable. Notice that the translation above refers to the ant as "she". In the new conservative Michelle Malkin' version the ant is "he". Now I have no idea what, in the original Greek, the pronoun is – and I'm not going to find out. What is interesting is that conservatives vacillate in their way of telling the story, in their account of the gender of the ant. That is one sign that they are talking of work, any work, all work, women's work, man's work: whoever you are, whatever you do, work is never done, is repetitious and not, in itself, of any interest to anyone.

 I suspect that the Biblical story of Adam and Eve remains behind how conservatives see our relation to work. Since the original pair, representatives of humanity, were booted from Paradise, they, we, are condemned to a life of hard toil. "Cursed shall be the ground because of you; in sorrow you shall eat of it all the days of your life. And thorns and thistles it shall bring forth for you, and you shall eat the plant of the field. By the sweat of your face you shall eat bread until you return to the ground." (Genesis, 3:17-19)

Work, nasty in nature as the conservatives see it, is the central feature of human lives.

Of course, there are always some people who for various reasons (the pre-lapsarian Adam and Eve, the village idiot as well as the Duke, the kept woman, those with large inherited wealth, and the devil of the conservatives, the layabout (see the grasshopper in the fable)) do not work. However, overwhelmingly people (including the traditional housewife doing her unremunerated tasks) do and must work. So first of all the ant in the fable is iconic for conservatives as it expresses that understanding of human life.

However, that work is a central feature of human lives is not anything that liberal, progressive, even radical opponents of conservativism deny.

What the conservative wildly overdoes, and what does merit scorn, is the comparison of very many human lives to the ant. The model for the ant's labors is the slave (which is what author of the fable was) or the assembly line worker, a very limited selection of the working lives of humans. Note: conservatives have not been found applauding the heroism of the assembly line worker or the sweatshop worker, though they do celebrate that kind of life when it comes to the ant. Is that not inconsistency?

Progressives must recognize this amount of truth in the conservative picture: there is much in most people's work that is drudgery, boring and destructive of the best in us. However, no matter how difficult work is generally, some employments are worse than others: and the fable chooses the most plodding of all as showing the real nature of work and of what it is to be human.

Do Michelle Malkin and company really think that they themselves are like the ant as they go about earning their daily bread? How many people do they know whose actual working lives are comparable to the ant? I wager: None. Yet they seemingly love Ant and generalize wildly from its life.

We should all recall that the left has (at least) two very excellent pieces of writing which do talk about the working lives of ordinary people: Studs Terkel's magnificent *Working* and Barbara Ehrenreich's *Nickled and Dimed*. We need to re-read those now.

The human analogs to the ant – where we ignore its postulated absolute solitude – are likely to form unions, to have formed unions, where workers can act to overcome the dreariness and worse of their working conditions. Do the conservatives applaud these attempts to rid working people of drudgery and worse? Of course not – such joint self-help organizations are anathema to the conservative. For the true hero is Ant who does not indulge in joining with others to help each other.

And that brings us to the second item in the conservative conception of work: the idea that work is always to be like the ant's labors (remember the curse placed on Adam and Eve) and we must not try to make it better.

Compare how the conservative thinks of the situation of the ant in Aesop's fable with what a progressive, a modern liberal, would say.

To the conservative, Ant is a hero for grindingly going on, day after day, with her/his labor. Work, conceived of as misery, is part of the very constitution of the universe and so it is something about which nothing can be done.

To the progressive such obnoxious styles of work as that of the assembly line, the sweatshop, the slave, the salary-man, child-labor and so on – the models for the conservative picture of work - are, in their various ways, capable of improvement, even elimination. It is assumed that we, both the progressive and the downtrodden workers, must rise up against that kind of labor, must join together to make their work and their lives better.

The conservative prefers hero-worship – the Heroic Ant - to joining together to eliminate or change obnoxious types of labor. (The ant of course has no fellows to band together with – and not even an employer to rise up against.) Again, while it is not part of conservative practice to actually praise workers who have lives like that of Ant, they ought to be doing that as a consequence of their outlook. The failure to love those who labor shows that it is the literary expression of the view that they love, not actual people who earn their daily bread in such ways.

The number of ways in which working life has improved for human analogs of the ant is too vast to catalog here (even if I could.) Let me insert something here from Charles Bayer.

Whether you are a fan of unions or you are not, all of us are far better off today because of the hard-fought victories they have won. Do you covet your right to work-free weekends? Then you must give organized labor the credit. American business did not agree to a forty-hour week out of a generous spirit. This right was the product of hard-fought organized power.

The lives of Americans (and Europeans and no doubt others too) are much better today because we progressives have supported and worked for changes in the nature of work, joining with those who do the work and who band together to change the way it is conducted. We progressives in solidarity with those who engage in the work have together achieved changes that the conservative conception of the place of work in the world assumes to be not possible.

The conservative conception of work embodied in the person (?) of Ant is flawed in at least three ways: it rests upon a picture of the nature of work (the model is the slave, the house maid or the assembly line worker) that is too narrow and thus does not accurately portray the variety of kinds of work that human beings engage in; it also represents work as unchangeable drudgery and refuses to see the vast improvements made in many people's work life over the past couple of hundred years and the possibilities for even more.

The third failure is this: the ant has no other life than work. In this conservative picture, life is work, there is nothing worth remarking on outside it. The ant has no social life, no television even, nothing to do after the daily fetching and carrying but wait for the next day with maybe a little laundry and house-cleaning tossed in.

The progressive vision includes the idea that there are other things in life than work that are humanly valuable and which need to be fostered both individually and socially. The liberal vision even includes the possibility that the work might someday be made not just less onerous (which has been happening now for a couple of centuries) but become not even the central feature of human life, to be replaced in importance by those other activities ignored or slighted by the conservative mind. It was one of the glories of the 1960's that that possibility was actively discussed. It is a theme that needs to be taken up again by progressives.

There are those who say 'Wait until we have returned to a settled economic condition before we start considering lives without work.' There is something to that: however, all those many people who presently are long-term unemployed, maybe now permanently so, might be brought to see that there is life not just after but without work (if you can get enough to eat.)

This completes the critical analysis of the ant in the fable – a question remains. Do contemporary conservatives, including those who are resurrecting Aesop's fable, really believe the conception of work found in the story? Or is just their hatred of Grasshopper that inclines them to mouth a more traditional conservative idea of the nature and place of work in human life? I have my suspicions that it is really the latter, that the so-called present conservatives are not really traditional conservatives at all except when it suits them.

So far, in looking into the fable of *The Ant and The Grasshopper*, I've been examining that hero of conservatives, the ant. What appeals to conservatives in that character is his or her atomism – the solitary figure going on with life without any supporting social institutions or even other 'people'. And what is that life the ant is leading? It is work: the ant embodies a conservative conception of life as unrelenting toil, accepted without demur.

Those conservative notions have been and should be the object of progressive criticism: we are not social atoms, the ant's style of work is not the model of all work and such work, even work itself, need not be accepted as a fact of human existence of such significance as the conservatives makes of it.

For the modern conservative, the ant, while embodying their conception of human life as work, is not the main attraction of Aesop's fable. Instead, it is the character of the grasshopper, so far not examined, that is the center of modern conservative attention. While it is likely that our future economic arrangements will make the notion of work again more central to conservative views, it is to their hatred of the grasshopper and what he stands for that we must now turn.

Note: whereas the ant, in the history of the fable, is sometimes thought of as male and sometimes as female, the grasshopper seems, at least in current thought to be male (though the expression 'welfare queens' does suggest that females can play the role as well.)

At the start, it is important to recognize that in the fable the grasshopper as well as the ant is conceived of as completely alone. There are no social institutions at all in the meadow – and the grasshopper is also not given any fellows. The idea of humans as fully formed solitaries – the Hobbesian picture – is crucial to the conservative love of the story, both in the character of the ant and that of the grasshopper as well. The individual in this view is completely responsible for whatever good or ill befalls them in the course of life.

Of course, there is a huge hole in the story at this point: how does the grasshopper support himself over the course of the summer? Perhaps he has caring friends or parents who, off-stage, bring him food daily. Those social institutions and other 'persons' missing in Aesop's story peek out from behind the structure here to remind us that the world is not as empty as the conservative myth has it.

The first thing to notice about the grasshopper is that when he is introduced into the story the initial contrast is between his attitude toward life and the ant's.

All day long she would work, without stop or rest, scurrying back and forth from the field, collecting the grains of wheat and storing them carefully in her larder. The grasshopper would look at her and laugh. 'Why do you work so hard, dear ant?' he would say. 'Come, rest awhile, listen to my song. Summer is here, the days are long and bright. Why waste the sunshine in labour and toil?' The ant would ignore him, and head bent, would just hurry to the field a little faster.

The grasshopper laughs – the ant nowhere is presented as laughing. Of course, in the evening as she contemplates the increasing stock of wheat in her larder, she may have a small feeling of satisfaction – but then she remembers that tomorrow is another day and tomorrow's work must be prepared for tonight. There is no laughter in the ant's world. I mentioned earlier that the song of Disney's dwarves in *Snow White*, 'Whistle while you work', is anathema to the conservative. Work is grim, life is without joy, with only small fleeting feelings of satisfaction when the current success of one's work is observed (though it may all fall apart tomorrow.) As Gary Wills noted in *Nixon Agonistes*, to the conservative character one must prove oneself anew every day: there is no resting on laurels, nothing more than a fleeting sense of today's job well done.

The grasshopper laughs both as an expression of joy at life, because of the beauty of the summer day and his engagement in the enjoyable activity of making music, but also laughs <u>at</u> the ant, for her incessant labor when she too could be enjoying the wonder around her. One may wish that the grasshopper had not laughed at Ant, but, hey, we progressives are human too.

On the other hand, the ant is presented as, in modern terms, a workaholic. There is no evidence given that she needs to be laying up that much for the hard times, that every minute of every day is consumed by a grim determination to keep working. But of course that attitude is an expression of the conservative idea that life is nothing but work.

The conservative criticism of the grasshopper in Aesop's fable rests upon several different features of his role. The grasshopper's joy in life, his cheerfulness and laughter, runs completely contrary to how the conservative urges us to see life: there is no (legitimate) joy in Mudville or any other place of human habitation.

There are (at least) two other major sources of distaste for the grasshopper, one obvious and one less so, one concerned with what he is not doing and one with what he is doing. Certainly the main theme is that the grasshopper is not working, is not gainfully employed, is not planning for the future. However, consider first what the grasshopper *is* doing.

He is making music all the day, day after day.

He could have been represented as say napping constantly, or as (in a modern version) watching trash TV or reading comic books, or perhaps canoodling with an equally unemployed lady grasshopper (or two). But that is not how he spends his time. Rather he makes music.

The grasshopper is a busker – though he doesn't even have his hat out for the passerby to drop in a coin or a grain of wheat in recognition of his providing enjoyment. At most he asks the ant to pause, listen and enjoy.

Let me generalize and say that he is practicing Art, musical art: though he might have been writing poetry or fiction, or painting. And we must think that the fable is condemning him for indulging in an artistic pursuit when he should have been doing something that might be intrinsically worthless but that does earn one money for doing it.

Toni Morrison, who has won both the Nobel and Pulitzer prizes for her novels, has taken the time to help create a (picture) book about the ant and the grasshopper. (Toni & Slade Morrison, pictures by Pascal Lemaitre, *Who's Got Game: The Ant or the Grasshopper?*) It is an engaging retelling of the fable in a modern urban setting: and the question posed for thought by the (young) reader is 'Should one pursue one's artistic dream or must one choose work?' A line in the book that calls for our attention is by the grasshopper: "How can you say I've never worked a day? ART IS WORK – it just looks like play."

Well, says the conservative, it is not gainful work. (Unless of course it is – some do get paid for their artistic endeavors.)

While I was looking up the Morrisons' book on Amazon, I came across an Amazon review of it by someone who signs themselves 'Responsible Artist (at work making money so I can eat AND make art!)' The review is a perfect expression of the conservative picture of artistic production versus gainful employment. "It's ok to have an appreciation for the arts. What's NOT ok is the author's message to kids that it's ok to completely cast aside your responsibility to provide for yourself in the pursuit of your dream of being an artist. What would have been a better twist on this story is that in the end the ant was not only a responsible citizen but an artist as well. I don't recommend this version. Stick with the original

Aesop's fable version. ART IS WORK but if nobody wants to buy it then you'd better be able to eat it."

We can be glad that the author does make the slight concession that art appreciation is "ok". Whoopee! But the author mistakes the Morrisons' message: it isn't that youthful readers are being encouraged to stick with their artistic dreams. Rather they are being asked to compare the two ways of life. Of course, in a world in which the views of Responsible Artist are the norm, the Morrisons try to give an equally strong voice to the other side. That is so far outside Responsible Artist's conservative vision of life that any encouragement to consider the pursuit of dreams as worthy of consideration can only be a recommendation to do so.

We more liberal people can try to think of all the various things that a young would-be-artist takes into consideration as they struggle with the problem of how to pursue their dream while needing to maintain themselves. Questions about the way they might live (would it suit them to be a hungry artist in a garret?), about how successful they might be as an artist, about whether economic conditions offer them a satisfying life outside art, about whether they can put together a life that involves working and saving for a while so that they can stop and return to what they want to do and so on. The conservative, embodied in Responsible Artist, isn't interested in those questions. Work first, then and only then think about whether you can find a way to do something artistic. Make money, live later!

Conservatives despise the grasshopper because he is so cheerful and because he spends his (summer) days doing something low on the scale of human activity, namely making music, especially as he is not providing for himself, making money, but is fiddling the day away.

But of course what he is most despised for is that he is NOT WORKING. He is able bodied, fully capable of remunerative work, but chooses not to. He has not been laid off, is not the victim of economic hard times, is not between jobs: the conservative disapproves enough of people who find themselves in those circumstances. But the grasshopper has made the choice not to work at a paying job in good times and that for the conservative is morally abominable.

It is even worse: he is *enjoying* himself in making music, i.e. enjoying himself in not working. And by making music in the meadow, along the path where the ant trudges many times a day, day after day, he is tempting the virtuous ant away from the path of righteousness. And in the fable he goes so far as to try to get the ant to stop that blind drive to acquire, to live a grim life, to stop and enjoy the day:

The grasshopper would look at her and laugh. 'Why do you work so hard, dear ant?' he would say. 'Come, rest awhile, listen to my song. Summer is here, the days are long and bright. Why waste the sunshine in labour and toil?' The ant would ignore him, and head bent, would just hurry to the field a little faster. This would make the grasshopper laugh even louder. 'What a silly little ant you are!' he would call after her. 'Come, come and dance with me! Forget about work! Enjoy the summer! Live a little!' And the grasshopper would hop away across the meadow, singing and dancing merrily.

Tempting the ant to avoid work and thus away from the virtuous life makes the grasshopper even more evil in the conservative world view.

Now let's think a bit. The ant is busy gathering the grains of wheat and storing them away for the season when the crop is finished. But surely during the summer she is consuming some of the wheat to keep herself going. Every night a little bowl of Cream of Wheat for dinner. However, the conservative version of the story doesn't even allow the grasshopper that much: yet surely the question must come up: How does the grasshopper survive the summer? Does he have parental support for his artistic endeavors? Do his friends supply him with the wherewithal to live during the good times? Has he worked, saved up and then quit in order to develop his musical abilities, living on what he saved? Did he inherit money? (The conservative suspects that he is drawing welfare benefits of some sort, enabling him to avoid work.)

It is just here that my earlier analysis of the conservative picture of human life, that it consists and must consist of work, becomes relevant. Work is not enjoyable – that is why the ant can be tempted even if heroically she overcomes the human temptation to not work, to avoid the necessary grind of acquiring one's daily bread, and thereby becomes even more morally virtuous. The grasshopper makes a choice to avoid the lot of humanity: and surely, for the conservative, a righteous universe will see to it that that choice is punished. And so we near the end of the tale.

There is one last piece of Aesop's fable to be considered, its conclusion, a conclusion that is dear to the conservative's heart.

Summer faded into autumn, and autumn turned into winter. The sun was hardly seen, and the days were short and grey, the nights long and dark. It became freezing cold, and snow began to fall. The grasshopper didn't feel like singing any more. He was cold and hungry. He had nowhere to shelter from the snow, and nothing to eat. The meadow and the farmer's field were covered in snow, and there was no food to be had. 'Oh what shall I do? Where shall I go?' wailed the grasshopper. Suddenly he remembered the ant. 'Ah - I shall go to the ant and ask her for food and shelter!' declared the grasshopper, perking up. So off he went to the ant's house and knocked at her door. 'Hello ant!' he cried cheerfully. 'Here I am, to sing for you, as I warm myself by your fire, while you get me some food from that larder of yours!' The ant looked at the grasshopper and said, 'All summer long I worked hard while you made fun of me, and sang and danced. You should have thought of winter then! Find somewhere else to sing, grasshopper! There is no warmth or food for you here!' And the ant shut the door in the grasshopper's face.

Let us suppose that matters in the meadow are just as the conservative has claimed: Ant has worked the summer away without deviating from the daily routine of collecting and storing the (farmer's) wheat away in her larder, never giving in to the temptation offered by the grasshopper to join him in song and dance; Grasshopper was fully capable of working throughout the long summer days as did Ant and was not out of work because of a seriously distressed economy or some other state of the economy, but instead chose to make music, no doubt an enjoyable activity but one that produced no income. Fall and winter come and Grasshopper has no food saved for the hard times. Starving, he turns to the ant for assistance (in the fable, there is no one else in the meadow to turn to.)

As we see, Ant tells the truth (from her conservative point of view) about what has happened over the summer, slams the door in the grasshopper's face, leaving him, without question, to his (supposed) deserts, to starvation. Grasshopper needs the good-will of the ant – she refuses to give it. (Though notice that Grasshopper does offer to pay for food – he will make music which he continues to assume the ant will enjoy.)

There is no doubt that the conservative psyche loves this result: you will get no help from me for the outcome is exactly what you deserve, the result of your own choices about how to live, so accept the suffering.

What is the liberal to say? Let us make the case most difficult for our side. Suppose that the critique (produced earlier in this analysis) of the conservative position on all the issues that arise about the circumstances in the meadow is ignored and that consequently we let the conservative have the correct interpretation of those circumstances. The liberal still has to strongly object to the ant's behavior. For in the ant's behavior, and the conservatives' approval of it, is an unrelenting nastiness packaged as morality.

There is absolutely no mercy shown or to be shown. Recall that Grasshopper has not harmed anyone else or the meadow, has not pillaged and plundered or savaged the local environment, but has simply not worked and not saved, has probably been irresponsible. He should be shut out to freeze to death for <u>that</u>? He deserves starvation for <u>that</u>?

It is not as if there is so little in the ant's larder that should she share it with the grasshopper, she will herself starve or even struggle to make it through the winter. She can well afford to help the grasshopper. But she doesn't – and the conservative will say she shouldn't. Conservative justice demands that.

What the conservative needs to be reminded of here is Portia's famous speech in *The Merchant of Venice*:

'"The quality of mercy is not strain'd,
It droppeth as the gentle rain from heaven
Upon the place beneath: it is twice blest;

It blesseth him that gives and him that takes:
'Tis mightiest in the mightiest: it becomes
The throned monarch better than his crown;
His scepter shows the force of temporal power,
The attribute to awe and majesty,
Wherein doth sit the dread and fear of kings;
But mercy is above this sceptered sway;
It is enthroned in the hearts of kings,
It is an attribute to God himself;
And earthly power doth then show likest God's
When mercy seasons justice. There, Jew,
Though just be thy plea, consider this,
That, in the course of justice, none of us
Should see salvation: we do pray for mercy;
And that same prayer doth teach us all to render
The deeds of mercy...."

Shylock has justice on his side (as we are assuming for now that the ant and does). However, there is something else to humanity. Even assuming, quite in the face of the correct account of life in the meadow, that justice is on the ant's side, there is an unmitigated Shylockian demand for justice, for rendering what one deserves regardless of the suffering caused by that demand.

That is not the way the liberal sees human life. As Portia says 'Mercy cannot be forced', cannot be required by law. But mercy is a moral virtue absent from the conservatives' narrow repertoire, from their view of life.

The traditional conservative loves Ant and dislikes Grasshopper and probably believes the entire fable is an expression of the way things are.

The contemporary conservative probably has less love for Ant, but her or his attitude toward Grasshopper has degenerated from disliking to despising.

However their entire picture of the world, of life, of work, of judgment of our fellow human beings is mistaken on all counts.